Books by Luis d'Antin van Rooten

Mots d'Heures : Gousses, Rames

The Floriculturist's Vade-Mecum of Exotic and Recondite Plants,
Shrubs and Grasses . . . and One Malignant Parasite

Luis d'Antin van Rooten

VAN ROOTEN'S BOOK OF IMPROBABLE SAINTS

An Irreverent Hagiography

Grossman Publishers
A Division of The Viking Press
New York
1975

First published in 1975 by Grossman Publishers
625 Madison Avenue, New York, N.Y. 10022

Published simultaneously in Canada by
The Macmillan Company of Canada Limited

SBN 670-74282-1
Library of Congress catalog card number: 75-21532

Printed in U.S.A.

2/06
gift

To
Juan Rodriguez and
Ricardo de Torre,
Bartenders,
who filled the glasses
George Melville Cooper, John Call,
and other fellow Players have
raised with me for no
earthly reason.

"Hallelujah!"

   —*St. Hark, the herald angel*

Foreword

"When the roll is called up yonder . . ."

Hagiology is not the science of the geriatrics of witches. It is the study of the lives of the saints. How I became interested in this field of arcane knowledge is quite simple. When I became an actor I discovered that the patron saint of thespians was St. Genesius. My curiosity aroused, I reached for my copy of *A Biographical Dictionary of the Saints,* by the Rt. Rev. F. G. Holweck, Domestic Prelate to His Holiness Pope Pius XI (1924). I indulge myself in this bit of gratuitous pomposity to indicate the extent and catholicity of my reference library. It does not include, however, the exhaustive and exhausting *Acta Sanctorum* of the Jesuit Bollandists of Belgium. I was amazed to discover that St. Genesius is traditionally believed to have suffered martyrdom in Rome, under the auspices of Diocletian, cira and circus, A.D. 303. His legend parallels in detail that of St. Gelasius of Heliopolis. My august authority concludes, "Perhaps the Western St. Genesius is identical with St. Gelasius of Heliopolis." The poor (how often, O Lord!) actors live out their lives of make-believe under the protection of a possibly make-believe saint. This doesn't seem to bother them very much and certainly it has never hurt anyone.

The true history of the saints is blurred by legend and the mists of time. Hagiologists and hagiographers are hard put to it to determine whether a saint is real or spurious, a legendary Christian or a heretic, or even the invention of some early devoted romancer. The Rt. Rev. Holweck says in his preface: "To separate as far as possible the genuine saints from those who are spurious, I have marked with an asterisk all persons found only in the separate churches and of whom it is not certain that they were in communion with the Apostolic See." The asterisks run through this book like the Milky Way across the heavens on a clear winter night. Some of the names I found, in passing, were as strange as their stories; for instance, St. Euphosynus of Pskow, St. Euschemon, St. Llwydog (of whom nothing is known), St. Mwchwdw or Bwchwdw (a forgotten Welsh saint), St. Gleb Andrejewitsh, and St. Dyfryg.

There are many veterans, living or tragic casualties, who merited the Victoria Cross, the Congressional Medal of Honor, or the Légion d'Honneur, who never received these decorations because there were no surviving witnesses to their heroic deeds. For the same reason, I believe there are many individuals in Paradise who remain anonymous, unheralded, and unsung.

The Holy See endows certain saints with the patronage of a specific country, city, profession, or occupation, etc., etc. Here again popular custom and tradition attribute certain qualities to particular saints. A votive candle is lit to St. Anthony of Padua for the recovery of a lost, strayed, or stolen article of personal value. St. Paschalis of Baylon, the official patron of Eucharistic congresses, is the beloved and revered patron of the kitchen in Mexican homes. A radio unit of the Signal Corps, U.S. Army of the Pacific, in World War II, elected St. Joan of Arc as their patron, because she, too, heard voices.

On the basis of the stated facts and fancies I can see no reason why I cannot invent my own haloed host, without disrespect or irreverence, and I hope to a good purpose.

The only true alcoholic I have ever known well was a brilliant director and charming gentleman whose only fault was a firm belief in plenary indulgence. I owe him a great deal professionally, and I learned from his example that alcohol and one's work do not mix. He kept an imaginary snake in his desk drawer and periodically would allow himself to be bitten so that he could reach for a goodly dollop of snake medicine, made of West Virginia corn. This simple expedient kept him in a perpetual state of Euphoria, U.S.A., and seemed to justify his desire to fall into mortal ginning. Psychologists and A.A. researchers have observed that people who use alcohol for religious or ceremonial purposes are less likely to become immoderate in their use of liquor. Therefore, I submit herewith a list of saints to be toasted, one for each week of the year. Naturally all legal holidays, holy days, birthdays, anniversaries, and other special occasions take precedence. That still leaves plenty of otherwise insignificant opportunities to raise a glass to a mythical saint and thereby make a meaningful rite out of a meaningless gesture. It is in this spirit that I offer these spirits for your spiritous consideration. Here's how!

Table of the Content

Van Rooten's
Book of
Improbable Saints

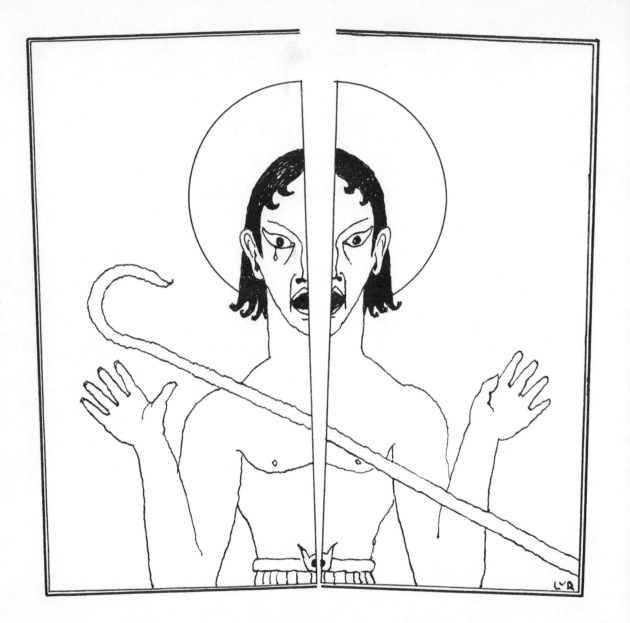

St. Dichotomy of Crete

The calendar year unfortunately does not divide itself exactly into fifty-two weeks; there is always something left over. Consequently, New Year's week is often, as is said in show business, a split-week engagement. To cover this fractionization at either end there is no more perfect protector than St. Dichotomy. Born in Crete in the IIId century, he was a devout and simple peasant patiently following his herd of goats over the mountainous terrain of his native island. One day he was surprised by a marauding band of infidel Turks, whose leader promptly cleft Dichotomy from crest to keel in one fell sweep of his damascene scimitar. Patron saint of schizophrenics. Special observance in Minneapolis and St. Paul and Buda-Pest. Candles and special devotions in times of ambivalence.

St. Philtre and Ste. Phine

Of Roman origin, St. Philtre spent much of his life in France. An inveterate evangelist and missionary, he would most often choose to preach in the cafés of large cities, where he was assured of a more or less captive audience. An intemperate band of ruffians finally drowned him out, in a manner of speaking, in a large coffee urn. He is often associated with Ste. Phine, who is of a much earlier vintage. Born in the Cognac region, she spent most of her life in Paris. A distilled spirit of great purity, she earned a meager living as a servant in a tavern. Sometime in the XVIIIth century they were adopted as the patron saints of coffee shops and bistros.

St. Apocrypha

One of the earliest of legendary saints, St. Apocrypha was a prolific writer and editor. Among some of the works attributed to him are the Acts of Pilate, the Gospel of Nicodemus, the Gospel of the Infancy, and Howard Hughes' memoirs. Because of the mythical character of his existence none of his works is included in official Church literature. His output was fabulous, making pikers of Arnold Bennett and Simenon. Many believe that, like Homer, he never existed, and that works attributed to him were really written by St. Anonymous, scrivener. I disagree, since anything that has a name must have a being, even if only imaginary. Patron of writers of fiction and other unsupported trivia.

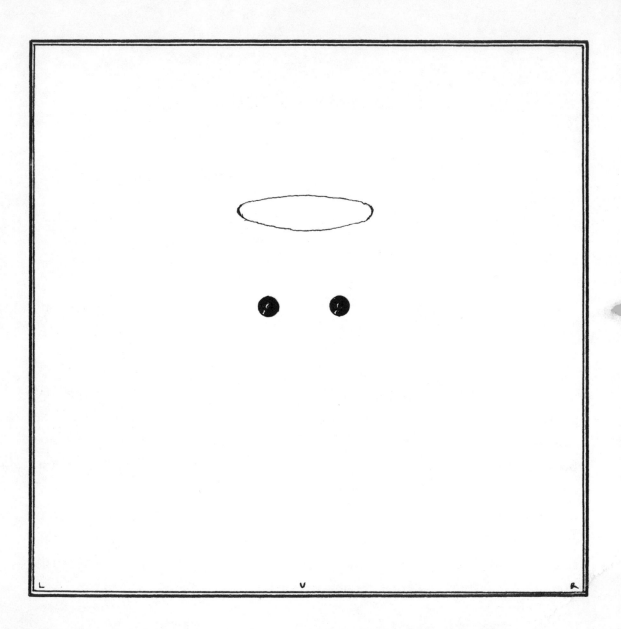

St. Umlaut of Ülzen, Lüneborg

A German hermit, St. Umlaut still holds the record for bouts of prayer, penitence, and fasting. His life was a long ululation of despair at the sins of the world. So rigorous were the disciplines to which he subjected himself, that his body became a transparent shadow. His burning black eyes have been reported to resemble two dots floating in space, without any apparent support. Nothing is known of his death, but legend holds that a heavenly breeze blew him away, leaving his eyes behind, like the Cheshire Cat's grin. Patron and protector of those suffering from attenuated vowels and ophthalmic goiter. Special dispensation for repeating St. Umlaut's prayer, "Grüss Gott," at the end of daily devotions.

St. Rose and St. Crimson Madder

Born to a deeply rooted Austrian family, St. Rose and St. Crimson were twins. From earliest infancy they demonstrated marked religious leanings and artistic tendencies. At a very early age they entered the Capuchin orders. St. Crimson became deeply involved in the illumination of manuscripts, and St. Rose took part in the painting of religious subjects that graced the altars of her convent chapel. Both high-complexioned redheads, they added a pleasing touch of color to their otherwise drab habits. Their works are unmistakable but unsigned. Patrons of painters, they are often invoked by watercolorists before a salon showing.

St. Francis T'sing T'song

Converted to Catholicism by Franciscan monks accompanying Marco Polo, Tung T'sing T'song was baptized Francis, in honor of the founder of the famous order. He remained in China, preaching the Gospel and teaching his followers his own translations of Roman liturgy. He was cut off in mid-hymn by the sword of an officer of the Imperial Guard. Patron of the humdrum. Special protector of the primary grades in European schools.

VII

St. Coleslaw of Lwow

Nothing whatsoever is known of this humble Polish truck gardener, except the extraordinary method of his martyrdom. He was condemmed to death by gradual decapitation. His relics were hidden in a pickling vat by his followers, but were later scattered all over Europe by the many invaders of Poland during the intervening centuries. Patron of salad-makers. Special devotions in delicatessens.

VIII

The Nine-and-a-Half Martyrs of Kamakura

Among the earliest converts to Catholicism in Japan, these nine men and a beggar girl named Keiko became lay missionaries in their own land. Keiko had been run over by a samurai's chariot and had lost both legs at the hips, thereafter propelling herself on a small wheeled platform. This explains their curious arithmetical nomenclature. Angered by their preaching of what he considered a heathen belief, the Emperor ordered that they should be thrown to the tigers in the Imperial menagerie. It is averred that the Emperor exclaimed, "Let them eat Keiko!" or "They can have their Keiko and eat them, too!" Historians cannot agree on exactly which. Special devotions, granting a year's indulgence, take the form of a baker's novena. Special observances in the Eastern Division of the American League for protection against marauding tigers.

IX

St. Mead the Saxon

St. Mead was a beekeeper who discovered the fermenting qualities of honey. His brews were extremely popular in medieval England. His generosity in sharing his product with all comers gave rise to the well-known saying, "One man's mead is another man's potion." He is said to have died of an acute attack of hives and his body was transmogrified into a bee. His spirit is still with us. Patron of apiaries. Special observance at wassails.

X

St. Calico of Madras

Many authorities claim St. Calico is a pure fabrication. At the same time, they cannot deny that St. Calico has replaced St. Phlax of Ireland in many instances. In the modern world he has, in turn, been replaced by a truly ersatz saint, believed to be of American origin, St. Polly Esther. It is probable that his legend has, as it were, been cut out of whole cloth. Patron of weavers and shirtmakers.

XI

St. Primogeniture and St. Entail

A Celtic farmer of humble origins, St. Primogeniture was a faithful follower of Christ. He prospered mightily and the envious Roman invaders put him to death. Since he died intestate his holdings reverted to the State and his relics were divided equally among his heirs. His son St. Entail had but a short tenure on life. He, too, suffered martyrdom and his relics were scattered on the Common ground. Known in the locality of their birth as SS. Gavelkind and Socage, they are special co-patrons of landowners and of wills, deeds, and testaments.

XII

St. Cedric Bongo

A convert who eventually entered the priesthood, St. Cedric Bongo remained as a missionary in his native Congo. His great penchant for percussion instruments led him to the innovation of chanting the Psalms to a finger-drum accompaniment. He is the first and probably the only man to have transmitted the beatitudes on a jungle drum. While setting the Old Testament to the rhythm of three drums, two cymbals, and a large gong, he was beaten to death with his own drumsticks by irate pagan neighbors. His innovations and techniques, however, were brought to the Caribbean by his followers. From there they have spread throughout the known world. Patron of percussionists and the beat generation.

XIII

St. Philibeg

All that is known of this Scots saint is that he lived a threadbare existence of which the pattern is a tissue of legend. My one reliable source, a devout Scots scholar of my acquaintance, could only say, "Och, the puir sweet mon, he was kilt."

St. Metastasis

Probably the most remarkable mystic in this limited calendar of saints, St. Metastasis grew up on a farm in the transalpine district of Switzerland. From earliest childhood she was given to religious ecstasies, resulting in cataleptic comas. During these episodes her soul would seem to leave her body, and she was identified, reincorporated, in many distant and varied locations, where she would perform good deeds and miracles. One day, according to legend, she was transmuted into a dove and flew off into the wild blue yonder. Patron of aeronauts and television. No known relics, obviously.

Ste. Maladie Endémique du Foie

France has given many remarkable saints to the church: Ste. Geneviève, St. Louis, St. Denis, Ste. Jeanne d'Arc. One cannot ignore, however, Ste. Maladie. She is known to every French man and woman. There have been many learned disputations about her name. To begin with, the Endémiques traced their ancestry to Endemix the Gaul, often called the Gall, because of the bitterness of his character. "Maladie" is supposed to be a corruption of the English "M'Lady," the name having been given to her by her Norman godfather. The "Foie" is sometimes spelled "Foi," which is more appropriate, and also "Fois," which is a large and distinguished French family (when still living with her fertile clan Maladie was, of course, called M'lle Fois by neighbors). Legend tells us that she caused a spring to flow from a rock, like Moses at Meribah, in Les Baux, a somewhat arid village in Provence. Patron of spas. Special veneration at Vichy, Aix-les-Bains, Baden-Baden, Pau, White Sulphur Springs, and Marienbad. Her relics were burned in the 1500s by the Huguenots.

St. Ultroneous

St. Ultroneous was never baptized but was a voluntary Christian. As to his life, there have been witnesses, not cited, but giving testimony. He may be said to be an anonymous but willing saint. Nothing else can be attested to.

XVII

St. Greggory of Stylus

Very few saints of the Coptic church are recognized by the Holy See. Therefore, Egyptian saints are rare indeed. A great schism developed in the Vth century over the concept of Monophysitism, finally declared a heresy by the Council of Chalcedon (A.D. 451). In the VIIth century, in an attempt to heal the breach, Heraclius advanced the proposition of Monotheletism in his *Ecthasis* (A.D. 638). He was helped in collating the tremendous collection of arguments and theory by an Egyptian scribe named Paraph, whom we know today as St. Greggory of Stylus. Initially, the inventor of a method of shorthand using only the beginnings of words, he proved to be of inestimable value to his master. He also never wavered in his allegiance to Rome. Patron saint of court stenographers and private secretaries. Special devotions by editors of digests. Relics unintelligible.

XVIII

St. Cedilla Onderzee

Born in the small village of Cofferdam, Holland, St. Cedilla was an attractive child, endowed with the stubbornness and firm determination of her people. Late one evening, while taking a stroll, she discovered a hole in the dike that held back the sea. Again, in an act characteristic of her people, she, without a second thought, stuck her finger in the hole to stop the flow of water. In her case, her finger just made the hole bigger, and soon a torrent was flowing through the dike. The dike disintegrated and the village of Cofferdam and the surrounding countryside were engulfed. St. Cedilla, however, was spared; through divine intercession she was able to exist under the sea. She became the St. Francis of the sardines of the pelagic world. On days of great calm, fishermen have observed a trail of bubbles rising mysteriously from the bottom. This phenomenon is regarded as a sign that St. Cedilla is keeping watch over, or, as it were, under, the vessel. Patron of submarine crews. Special devotions in times of shipwreck, floods, tidal waves, and typhoons.

XIX

San Risotto il Milanese

A scullery boy in the home of a prominent Milanese family, San Risotto also served as an altar boy in the city's famous cathedral. Occasionally allowed to help in the preparation of the elaborate cuisine of the period, he soon became, by studious application and fervent prayer, an excellent chef. One fatal year, drought destroyed the crops and left Milan suffering from famine compounded by an epidemic of the plague. San Risotto was one of the few spared, and on his frail shoulders fell the burden of caring for and feeding his master's family and his fellow workers. Miraculously, the larders of the palazzo were replenished every night, and there was enough food for the family and for the hundreds of hungry citizens that came to the kitchen door. His grateful master was going to make him the principal chef of the household, but a jealous co-worker strangled poor San Risotto and expertly carved him into small grain-like pieces, which he promptly disposed of down the palazzo drains. No relics were ever recovered. Patron of North Italian restaurants.

São Trespuntos

A Portuguese Dominican who accompanied the Second Crusade to Asia Minor. Wandering off by himself one day, seeking solitude for meditation and prayer, he was set upon by a band of marauding Saracens. Without a trial they condemned him to death by drawing, quartering, and beheading. They had just begun their bloody work when a band of Christian knights appeared and drove them off. Alas, they were too late; São Trespuntos had died in the middle of an interrupted sentence. There is no record of what came after.

XXI

Santa Dolores de Cabeza

A noble Spanish family, the Cabezas are said to have been related on the distaff side to Alvar Núñez, Cabeza de Vaca. They followed this intrepid explorer to the New World in a viceregal retinue and were given a royal grant in what is now the state of Hidalgo. It was at their Hacienda Malatesta, named for an Italian connection, that Dolores gave her first cry. She was educated in all the proper arts and crafts of a daughter of a wealthy family and learned to read and write by eavesdropping; her brothers had a tutor in these masculine accomplishments. She entered a Carmelite convent and devoted herself to the composition of rhapsodic religious poems. She died when she was struck on the head by a loose tile that fell from the convent chapel roof. All her literary work was destroyed during the XIXth- and XXth-century revolutions. Patron of lyric poets. Special devotions for migraine sufferers. Relics scattered by Juarist anticlericals.

XXII

St. Triglyph and St. Echinus

Mentioned in a lost epistle to the Corinthians, these saints belonged to the Doric and Ionic orders, respectively. They imposed upon themselves the penance of capital punishment, made popular by St. Simeon Stylites. They spent their lives in meditation and prayer on top of twin columns. Cousins of St. Ovolo, St. Cyma Recta, and St. Entasis. Patrons of flagpole sitters and penthouse dwellers.

XXIII

St. Petroleum

Of the earth, St. Petroleum is a truly fabulous saint. Many men have gone broke in an attempt to find some trace of him. He is known all over the world. The credibility of his legend is proven by the fact that many of the faithful have adopted his name, notably Petroleum Vesuvius Nasby, American journalist and satirist (1833–1888). Patron of well-riggers and refineries; patron of Tampico, Mexico, and Oil City, Pennsylvania. Special veneration in many parts of Texas and the Middle East.

XXIV

San Transverso Colón

An obscure Spanish abbot, San Transverso is reputed to have been an avuncular ancestor of Cristóbal Colón, who discovered the New World. There is no doubt that this close religious connection did much to influence Isabella the Catholic in her support of the great Admiral of the Ocean Sea. If the *Santa María*, the *Niña*, and the *Pinta* had foundered in mid-Atlantic, the chances are that San Transverso would have joined the company of forgotten saints. Special devotions in cases of peptic ulcers. Patron of naval cadets and citrus growers. Relics at Bajo Estómago, Estremadura, Spain.

XXV

St. Bayou of Okefenokee

More commonly known as the "Water Lily of the Everglade," this modest Seminole maiden was among the first converts of the Franciscans who accompanied the expeditions of Ponce de León. When she returned home and tried to explain her enlightenment, her father tossed her into the nearest swamp. She sank into the muck up to her knees, head first, and then disappeared. Relics under the Tamiami Trail. Special devotions during periods of drought. Patron of sloughs. Much spiritual grace can be gained by murmuring, when raising a glass, the ejaculation, "O.K. Bayou."

XXVI

St. Brewis Llwllwlly

St. Brewis was a wandering Welsh minstrel who enjoyed much fame and popularity until he began singing Psalms. His wild compatriots promptly tossed him into a cauldron of water and boiled him alive. Nothing else is known about him except that he was quite young—a mere broth of a boy, as the Irish would put it. As *we* might say, he ended up in the soup.

Sancta Pietra di Rognoni

On the stony slope of the Apennines, on either side of the ridge, were the twin villages of Rognoni. The villagers scratched out a bare existence in their hard-to-reach fields. They finally abandoned their sterile lands and migrated to the plains. Only one remained behind—Sancta Pietra. We do not know whether she was born on the eastern or western slope. We do know that she was a simple peasant woman, with a faith as firm as the rock on which her home was built. She lived as a hermit until her death, which resulted from a gradual petrification of her body. She was buried in the village church, and then the miracles began, along with the gradual disintegration of the villages. The legendary site still remains as a shrine for pilgrims, particularly those suffering from nephritis and other dorsal complications. Patron of masons specializing in the construction of ribbed arches and groined vaults.

XXVIII

Sancta Pasta di Paestum

This saint has created a great controversy among hagiologists. Some are convinced she came from China with Marco Polo, while others are convinced that her antecedents were absolutely native to Italy. Like most controversies, it is an emotional rather than an intellectual difference of opinion. The fact remains that this saint is an integral part of southern Italian life. A ubiquitous saint, she often appears before the faithful, accompanied variously by St. Allium, SS. Burro and Pomodoro of Palermo, and St. Fromage of Lyons. Veneration before meals throughout southern Italy. Relics outside the walls of Naples.

XXIX

St. Kotwal of Java

St. Kotwal was a minor public official who had to keep his religion secret for political reasons. He sought the solitude of the coffee groves surrounding his native village to pray and meditate. Discovered by the owner of the plantation, he was promptly dispatched by a Malay kris to join the company of Christian saints. Patron of persecuted minorities.

St. Cothurnus

St. Cothurnus was a devout mystic who earned a meager living as a cobbler. His great interest in amateur theatricals inspired his invention of the buskin, a thick-soled boot reaching to the calf, thereby giving added height to the performers. During the enactment of a Passion play, while playing the role of the Saviour, he evinced the well-known phenomenon of the stigmata. He died in an out-of-town tryout of a new miracle play. Patron of cobblers, he should also, in my humble opinion, be the patron of actors on the road. Protector of Little Theater and Off-Broadway productions. Special devotions before opening nights.

XXXI

St. Pancreas

Roman martyr, 1st century A.D. Special veneration in Kidney, Australia, and County Spleen, Ireland. Relics transported to Londinium, now London, by Latin missionaries and buried in the crypt of a small chapel. The site is now occupied by a large railroad station, with the anglicized name of St. Pancras. The relics are supposed to be somewhere under the fourth platform. Patron of diabetics and those suffering from hypoglycemia. Votive chapel in Chatham, Massachusetts. Pilgrims are welcome; ask at the police station for directions.

XXXII

S. Seborrhea and S. Scrofula

These two daughters of prominent Italian families who had settled in Epidermis, Greece, lived very protected lives. They finally broke out and joined a group of pilgrims to Jerusalem. This turned out to be a rash undertaking. They were plagued by outbreaks of fever, eruptions of extinct volcanoes and finally died of acute sunburn in the desert of Erysipelas. They were anointed with holy oils and buried where they fell. Often confused with St. Urticaria and St. Acne. Patrons of those who lead blemished lives. Special veneration by individuals who can't come up to scratch.

XXXIII

St. Skagerrak the Viking

St. Skagerrak was the eldest son of St. Kattegat the Dane. Following the family tradition, he spent his life in extensive travels. He is said to have accompanied Leif Ericsson to the North American continent. He was converted to Christianity while trading in the Holy Land. He and his entire crew disappeared in the North Atlantic on their way to Greenland to preach the Gospel. Patron of those lost at sea.

XXXIV

St. Kastro the Bedouin

St. Kastro's nomadic life unfolds in the Arabian desert, India, and what is now Israel. Originally a Mohammedan, he became, during his wanderings in India, a follower of Buddha and then of Confucius. On his arrival in Judea he became deeply involved in Judaism and became a convert; from there it was but a step to Christianity. Because of his religious meanderings he earned the epithet, "The Convertible." Accustomed to riding a king-size, double-humped Bactrian, he fell off a single-humped dromedary, and the merciful shifting sands of the desert blanketed his remains. He sleeps in the unsullied wastes of Araby. Patron of insomniacs. Invoked on the arrival of unexpected guests. Patron of Sleepy Hollow, Mattress County, New York. Special observance at Mont Rêve, Chaiselongue, France. Annual novena at Bedford Springs, Pennsylvania.

XXXV

St. Pickip the Czech

St. Pickip's family name is so full of cees, zees, aitches, and kays and so few vowels that it is impossible to pronounce. It is generally ignored. A compulsive reader, he was very much impressed by Christ's advice to the wealthy young man. Being a man of some substance, he decided to take the advice seriously. He proceeded to give his money to the poor and to be extremely generous to his less fortunate friends. The whole business backfired. The poor spent the money in his shops, and he built up such enormous good will that he prospered more than ever before. He died a wealthy and beloved man. Patron of generous deeds and charitable acts. Special observance in places of public entertainment.

XXXVI

St. Vulgar and St. Vodka

St. Vulgar was a boatman who ferried travelers across the Dvina River. We find the legend of St. Christopher paralleled, in this instance, with a slight variation of detail. St. Vodka was a hermit who sustained herself by making and selling a liqueur of her own invention. It is said that weary travelers found her potion invigorating and refreshing. Both St. Vulgar and St. Vodka led miserable lives and died tragically in the best Russian literary tradition. Co-patrons of travelers in uninhabited regions. Recognized by the Coptic Church. For some inexplicable reason St. Vodka is associated and often represented with a Muscovite mule. St. Vulgar is referred to in a popular Russian hymn.

XXXVII

St. Mocha and St. Java

Arabic saints are comparatively rare, since their world is dominated by Islam. These two cousins, brought up together, were as inseparable as Siamese twins. They were converted by Dominican fathers accompanying the Third Crusade. With the stubborn fanaticism of their people they became recluses of the desert, vowing themselves to prayer, silence, and fasting. They subsisted on dates, and on special occasions they had coffee brought to them by admiring devotees, which coffee they abstemiously shared in one zarf and finjan. Their footprints and their lives were drifted over by the shifting sands of the Arabian desert. Special observance in Brazil and Colombia. Often invoked in breakfast devotions.

XXXVIII

St. Hyperbole

We know that as a young man he led an exaggerated and extravagant life. After his conversion he was given to long and complex sermons, more to impress than to be believed. He is known to have had some relation to the Asymptote sects. References to him can be found in the conic sections of some hagiographies. Legendary patron of hot-air balloonists.

St. Trilemma

This otherwise undistinguished saint was a Swiss, but whether of French, Italian, or German predilection has never been determined. He nearly created the first schism in the Roman church, by starting a controversy on the order of precedence in the worship of the Father, the Son, or the Holy Ghost. He fell into the Trappist order and left it to organize the Trilemmists. Their internal division led to what some considered worship of the profane, but it is known that St. Trilemma eventually brought all the monks back to the central, but never resolved, question. Their indecision quickly destroyed the order. Invoked at times of vacillation.

St. Borborygmus

A muffled rumble, a murmur on the breeze of legend, St. Borborygmus is entirely hearsay. Whence he came and went no one knows, but his existence echoes throughout history, into modern times. He is not to be denied. Invoked in cases of excessive flatulence. Patron of Buenos Aires, Argentina. Special observance in Gascony.

XLI

St. Penduline

An Albanian mystic, St. Penduline was first attracted by the teachings of St. Francis of Assisi, later by the austerities of St. Simeon Stylites. Unable to find an adequate column, she had herself swung in a net high in an oak tree in her native mountains. She spent her life in her leafy hammock, among her beloved birds, in prayer, fasting, and meditation. Patron of those doomed to die by hanging and other swingers.

XLII

The 10,000 Virgins of St. Ursula

The story of St. Ursula and her crusade of virgins, which ended so disastrously and tragically, is too well known to repeat here. The greatest miracle surrounding this event, however, is seldom commented upon. Considering the population of the Christian world at that time, and its mores, where did St. Ursula ever find 10,000 virgins? Co-patrons of activists, demonstrators, and the Women's Movement.

XLIII

St. Sarabanda

St. Sarabanda was a cousin of St. Sarinda, whom she greatly resembled. Born of a high-caste Indian family, she was given a liberal education. Of a marked musical bent, she became a Christian personification of Euterpe. Traveling extensively with her merchant father, her influence was felt everywhere she went. She is credited with being instrumental in introducing music into early Christian ritual. Her martyrdom is the first one recorded in which the victim was strangled with her own G-string. A band of heathen Kurds are held responsible. Patron of viola players.

XLIV

St. Lacustrine

The legend of St. Lacustrine has been borrowed, stolen, twisted, and elaborated by a plethora of authors from Sir Thomas Malory in *La Morte D'Arthur*, Tennyson in *Idylls of the King*, Sir Walter Scott in *The Lady of the Lake*, to James Branch Cabell (remember him?) in *Jurgen*. We are left with two sure attributes—a lake and a sword. Peacefully may she lie beneath its waters, wherever it is. Patron of lakes, pickerel, sunfish, and muskellunge. Special veneration at Lake Titicaca. Might be invoked to help the sad plight of Lake Erie.

San Policarpo Tapayaxin

Baptized Policarpo by Dominican missionaries, he is more familiarly known as St. Tapayaxin. He escaped to the desert to avoid slavery at the hands of the Spanish conquistadores. He lived as a hermit and was known for his strange power over lizards and snakes. They protected him from interruptions by interlopers when he was at prayer. Invoked against snake bite. Special devotions at the Culebra Cut, Panama Canal, Panama. He is venerated by descendants of the Chichimeca tribe, and is believed by them to be a descendant of Quetzalcoatl, the feathered serpent God.

XLVI

Saints Preserve and Protectus

That these two saints were converted and baptized by St. Patrick seems indubitable from the internal evidence. St. Patrick had spent many years in France, which explains why he gave one a French name, even though the other received a Latin one. Their legend is intertwined with Irish tradition, and they are, of course, jointly invoked with the ejaculation, "Saints Preserve and Protectus!" Relics preserved in a jar of poteen in the village church at Thatch, County Kilkenny, Ireland. Their portraits graced the tavern sign of the Sword and Shield in the same village. These have weathered away.

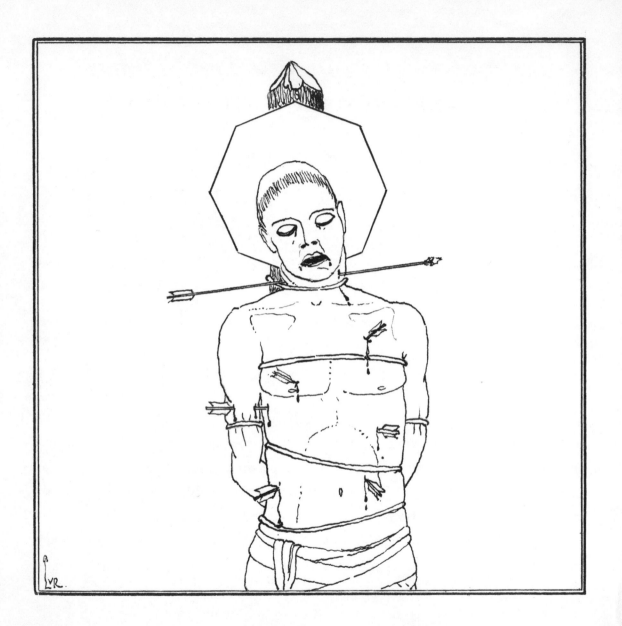

XLVII

St. Haven of Grace

When colonists first came to what is now Maryland, they brought a plentiful supply of blunderbusses, powder, and ball, in order to make friends with the natives. Almost as an afterthought they also brought along a missionary—St. Haven of Grace. As far as the Indians were concerned, they felt the neighborhood was deteriorating and started taking potshots at the invaders. They felt they needed target practice so they tied St. Haven to a stake marking the finish line of their ritual races. He died, a true martyr, of an overdose of flint arrowheads. His relics are reputedly buried under the finish post of a famous race track that bears his name, in French. He is the only saint depicted with an octagonal Baltimore aureole. Patron of archers, fletchers, and quiver-makers. Invoked during the racing season.

XLVIII

S.S. Haggis, Doch, and Dorris

Belonging to the same sect, these three ascetics lived in a turf hut on the Scottish heath. They subsisted on a blood pudding boiled in an old leather bagpipe sack and drank a brew cooked up by St. Doch and St. Dorris. St. Doch was extremely short and is often affectionately called Wee Doch by the faithful. Dour by nature and ancestry, the three saints would at times be inspired by the Water of Life and spend the night in loud singing of joyful hymns. The details of their lives and deaths are irrelevant in view of the fact that their influence is still felt in their native heath. Patrons of pipers and distillers. Invoked at all clan gatherings.

XLIX

St. Youdou the Voudou

Brought to Latin America as a slave from his native Africa, St. Youdou became a convert. His innate sense of rhythm and talent as a dancer soon made him a participant in the ritual dances performed by such as Fra Argentine Tango during the mass in olden days. The dance steps St. Youdou originated enjoyed a popular revival, both in Europe and North America, during the third decade of the present century. The grave mien of the adepts unmistakably indicated the religious source of their terpsichorean endeavors and inspired the French critical observation, *"La face qui s'ennuie, le cul qui s'amuse."* Patron of ballroom dancers and musicians. Invoked by gauchos on feast days.

Ste. Bourse de Bruges

Born in the XIVth century and brought up in the Venetian tradition, she became a Sister of Charity. Her financial talents soon earned her the post of almoner for her convent, and her great success soon made her a power in the European economy of the period. There is no doubt that she was responsible for the pre-eminence of Bruges as a religious and banking center in the Gothic world. Patron of stock-brokers, moneylenders, and charitable institutions. Invoked in times of financial stress, she is a saint of great interest.

St. Incunabula

A Carmelite nun, St. Incunabula was the librarian of her convent in Pergamum. She is best described in the words of William Shakespeare as "a snapper-up of unconsidered trifles." Her particular passion was the collection of fragmentary manuscripts, to which she gave her name. Noted for her translations, collations, and interpretations. Patron of librarians, manuscript collectors, and newspaper morgues. Special patron of the Dead Sea Scrolls.

LII

Sancta Penultima

Christian names seem to run in cycles of popularity. Dorothy, Laura, Jane, Anne, Elizabeth, Thomas, Cyril, Cuthbert, and Charles have all had their day. In the very beginnings of the Christian Era every girl child seems to have been called Mary, that grand old name. Such was the case of the saint we have under consideration. All we know is that she is alleged to have witnessed the Entombment. Then, like the woman taken in adultery, she is heard of no more. There is no question that she was deeply moved by the experience. Adopted by a devout group of Italians, she was called Sancta Maria della Pena Ultima—St. Mary of the Ultimate Sorrow. The horny hand of time has erased her first name and the preposition, and merged her epithet into one word—Penultima. So she remains to this day. Patron of usually ill-fated and long-suffering innocent bystanders and compulsive funeral-goers. Like St. Paschalis of Baylon, she is said to appear to persons about to die. Not a very cheerful saint.

LIII

St. Finis

Twenty-sixth and last child of a Cornish fisherman father and a Roman mother, who had been left behind in Britain by the Roman legions when they retired to the continent. He was born near Land's End and at his birth his mother exclaimed, *"Finis est."* Finis he became. He was affectionately called Finny by his father, who often took him on his fishing expeditions as a luck piece; many miraculous catches are recorded in his legend. One day they were caught in a sudden storm, and the boat foundered off the shore of Finistère, France. All hands were lost, except Finis, whose almost lifeless body was cast up on the strand. A kind Breton housewife tried to revive him with good Normandy calvados, but in her anxiety she picked up a flagon of furniture restorer by mistake. That polished poor Finis off. Relics at Land's End and Cape Finisterre, La Coruña, Spain. Patron of those lost at sea and of exceptional distilled liquors. Invoked by writers on terminating a literary work. The connection is obscure.

Hallelujah